# How the U.S. Government Works

## Third Edition

By Syl Sobel, J.D.

sourcebooks eXplore

## To Marissa,
## who asked me to write this book.

Published by Sourcebooks eXplore, an imprint of Sourcebooks Kids
P.O. Box 4410, Naperville, Illinois 60567-4410
(630) 961-3900
sourcebookskids.com

ISBN: 978-1-4380-1163-9

Library of Congress Control No.: 2018961886

Source of Production: Wing King Tong Paper Products Co. Ltd., Shenzhen, Guangdong Province, China
Date of Production: March 2023
Run Number: 5031092

Printed and bound in China.
WKT 10 9 8 7 6 5 4 3 2

# ★ TABLE OF CONTENTS ★

# ★ INTRODUCTION ★

**W**hy is there a government?

To answer this question, let's think about your school. Imagine what your school would be like if each class had different rules from the other classes, if each class made a schedule without coordinating with the other classes, or if the school had no principal.

What would happen if one class wanted to go to the library at 10 o'clock, but another class wanted to use the library at the

same time? Who would decide which class would use the library? What if some classes allowed students to have cell phones but others didn't? Would students bring their cell phones into some classes but have to leave them outside for others?

What if the school had no office staff, building custodians, or cafeteria workers? Who would keep track of attendance? Who would keep the building clean and the heat and air conditioning working? Who would make lunch and serve it to students?

Your school would be a pretty confusing place, wouldn't it?

That's what the United States was like in the 1780's. The thirteen states had just won their independence from Great Britain in 1783, and even though they called themselves "the United States of America," the states were not "united" and working together as one country.

Instead, each state was like its own separate country. Each state had its own rules—which are called *laws*—but there were very few laws that applied to all of the states. Each state had its own type of money, but there was no single type of money that all of the states accepted. That made it difficult for the people or *citizens* of one state to buy or sell things in other states.

In addition, some of the states were not getting along with each other. Some were fighting about borders and the use of rivers and other waterways, and there was no system for settling these disagreements. And, while individual states had their own armies to protect themselves, there was no army and navy to protect the entire country and no way to pay for one.

Leaders of the states realized that this wasn't working and that the new country needed to make laws that applied to all of the citizens of all of the states. They wanted one type of paper money and coins that could be used in every state, and a way to resolve disagreements between the states. They needed an army and a navy to protect the United States from other countries.

The states sent some of their wisest leaders and citizens to a meeting in Philadelphia to decide how to fix these problems. They decided that the country needed a *government*, called a *national government*, that could make laws, raise money, form an army

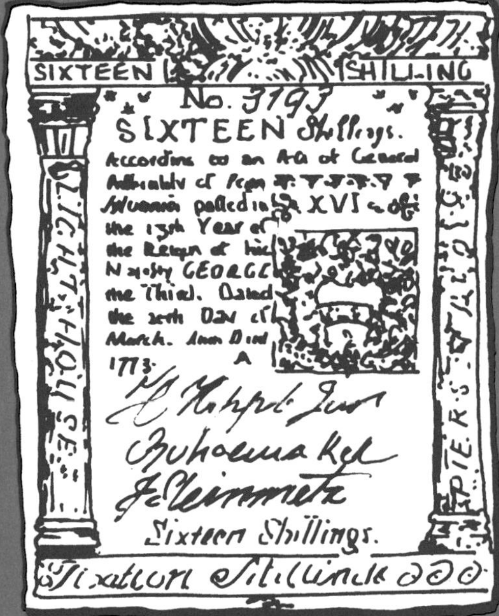


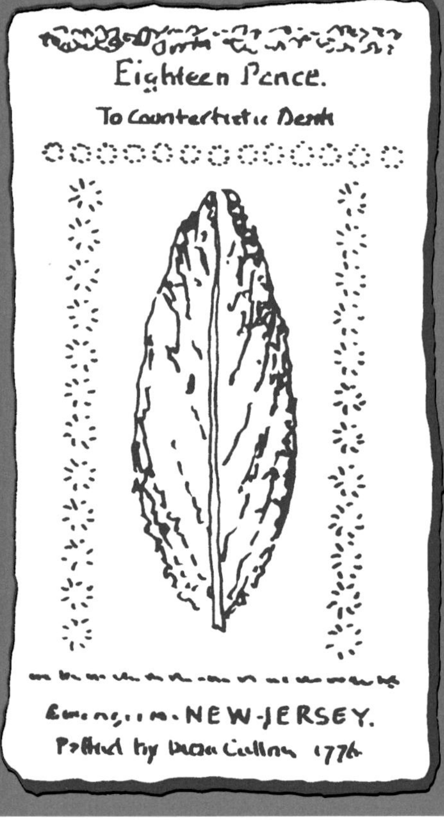


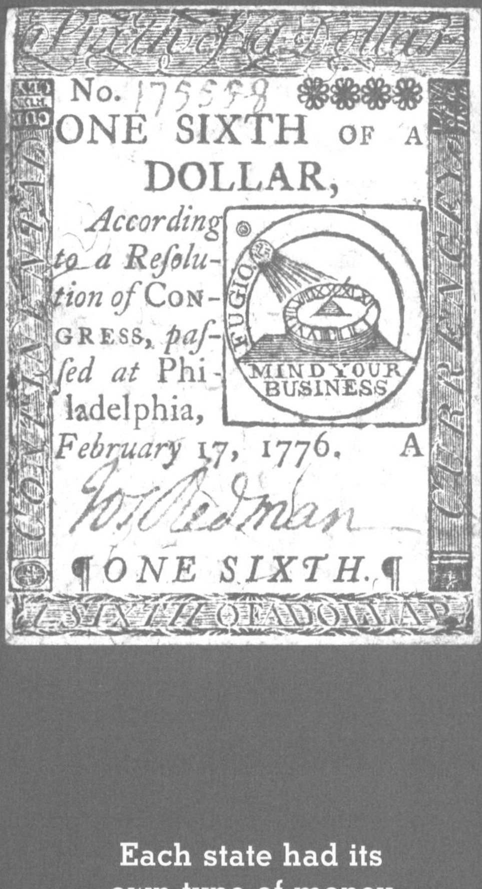


Each state had its own type of money

and navy, and do other jobs for all of the United States. They wrote a set of rules that defined the powers and responsibilities of the government. These rules are called the *Constitution of the United States*. The Constitution creates a type of government called a *republic,* which gets its power from the citizens. The citizens choose people to lead the government, who are called *representatives*.

## The Constitution says that the U.S. government has three main jobs:

- The first job is to make laws that apply to all of the states.
- The second job is to perform the many duties that the Constitution and laws of the United States say the national government should do. These duties include organizing and maintaining the army and navy, working with other countries, printing paper money and making coins that people could use in every state, building highways and bridges, and enforcing the laws, such as laws about public health and safety, banking, and the environment.
- The third job is to decide disagreements about the law. This includes deciding whether a person broke a law and how to punish people who did. It also includes resolving disputes between people and deciding what a law means when citizens disagree with each other or with the government about its meaning.

The Constitution divides the U.S. government into three parts called *branches* and gives each branch one of these jobs.

# We the People

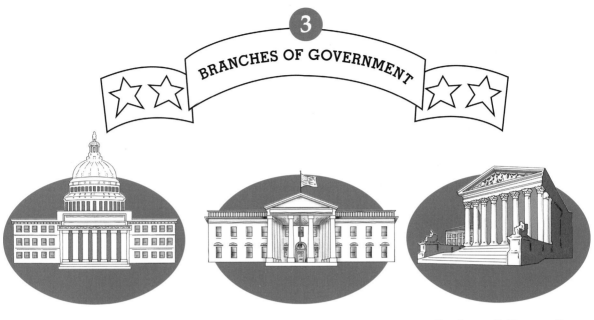

**Legislative Branch**　　　　**Executive Branch**　　　　**Judicial Branch**

 # The Legislative Branch

The first branch, called the *legislative branch*, makes the laws. The *Congress of the United States* performs the work of the legislative branch.

 # The Executive Branch

The second branch, called the *executive branch*, carries out the laws and is the biggest branch of government. The leader of the executive branch is the *President of the United States*. The president and people who work in the executive branch are responsible for performing the many jobs that the Constitution and the laws give to them. The president also commands the U.S. Army, Navy, Air Force, Marine Corps, and Coast Guard, which together are called the *military*, and represents the United States in meetings with leaders of other countries.

# 3 The Judicial Branch

The third branch, called the *judicial branch*, resolves questions about the law. The courts do the work of the judicial branch and decide many disagreements that people cannot settle between themselves. They decide whether people broke the law and how to punish them if they did. In addition, if the meaning of a law or a section of the Constitution is unclear, *courts* decide what it means.

The U.S. government did not replace all of the state governments. Each state still has its own government and its own laws. Each state has its own courts, too. However, the laws of the United States apply to everyone who lives in all of the states, while the laws of an individual state only apply to the people in that state.

**FOR DISCUSSION:** Sometimes people in some states want the U.S. government to make a certain law, but people in other states don't. What kind of laws do you think should apply to all of the people in all of the states? What kind of laws do you think should apply only to the people in a particular state?

# ★ THE CONGRESS ★

Congress makes the laws of the United States. Some laws tell the government what it is supposed to do. Other laws tell people and businesses what they can and cannot do. For example, some laws say it is a crime to steal money from a bank. Other laws protect our health and safety, such as laws that tell people who produce food what they must do to make the food safe to eat and laws that require seat belts and other safety equipment in cars.

Congress is made up of two groups, which are called houses. The two houses of Congress are the *U.S. Senate* and the *U.S. House of Representatives*. Citizens of each state who are 18 and older select men and women to represent their state in the Senate and the House of Representatives. They do this by voting in an *election*. A system of government in which citizens make decisions by voting is called a *democracy*.

The members of the House of Representatives serve in that job for two years, while the members of the Senate serve for six years. If they want to continue as representatives or senators, they must be elected again. The government holds an election for Congress every two years. At that time, all of the members of the House of Representatives and one-third of the members of the Senate are elected.

U.S. Capitol Building, Where Congress Works

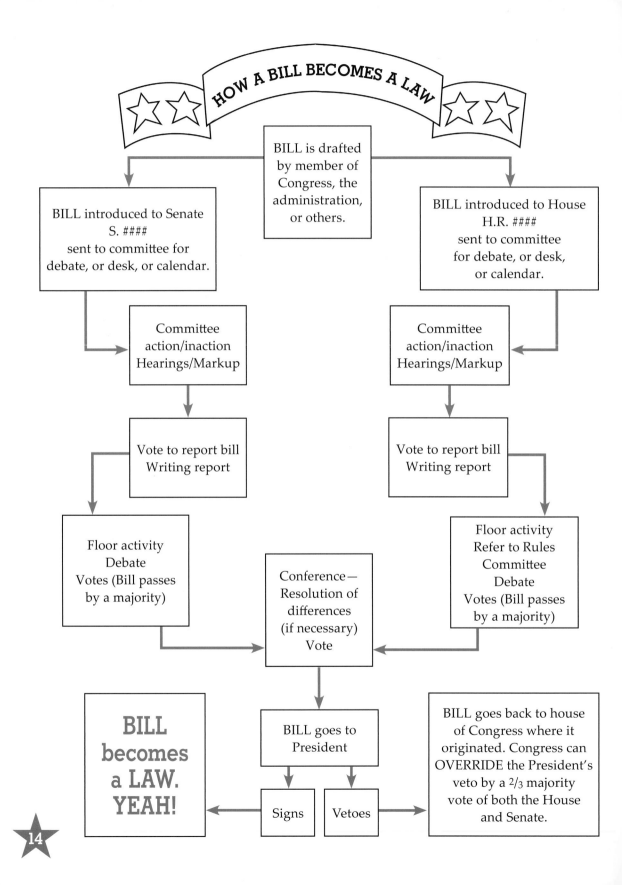

**HOW A BILL BECOMES A LAW**

BILL is drafted by member of Congress, the administration, or others.

BILL introduced to Senate S. #### sent to committee for debate, or desk, or calendar.

BILL introduced to House H.R. #### sent to committee for debate, or desk, or calendar.

Committee action/inaction Hearings/Markup

Committee action/inaction Hearings/Markup

Vote to report bill Writing report

Vote to report bill Writing report

Floor activity Debate Votes (Bill passes by a majority)

Floor activity Refer to Rules Committee Debate Votes (Bill passes by a majority)

Conference— Resolution of differences (if necessary) Vote

BILL becomes a LAW. YEAH!

BILL goes to President

BILL goes back to house of Congress where it originated. Congress can OVERRIDE the President's veto by a 2/3 majority vote of both the House and Senate.

Signs

Vetoes

**M**embers of Congress meet with each other often to discuss changes to current laws and ideas for new laws. Sometimes all of the senators meet, and sometimes all of the members of the House meet. Smaller groups called committees often meet, too. These meetings, and most of the work that Congress does, take place at the *U.S. Capitol* building in Washington, D.C.

## MAKING LAWS

When members of Congress want to suggest a new law, they prepare a written version of the law called a *bill*. The rest of the members of Congress can then read the bill, talk about it, suggest changes, and decide whether or not they want to make it a law. Members often do not agree on a bill because they have different ideas about what government should do and how it should do it. If enough members support the bill, Congress will vote on whether or not to make it a law.

When a majority of the senators and a majority of the representatives vote for a bill to become a law, then Congress sends it to the president. If the president agrees by signing the bill, then it becomes a law of the United States.

Sometimes, however, the president does not agree with a bill. If the president rejects a bill and sends it back to Congress without signing it, that is called a *veto* and the bill does not become a law. Congress can try again to make the bill a law despite the president's veto, but the Constitution requires both houses to pass the bill again by a two-thirds majority, which is sometimes called a *supermajority*.

A bill can also become a law if the president does not sign it and does not send it back to Congress within ten days. If, however, Congress has ended its meetings before those ten days are up, then the bill does not become a law. This is called a pocket veto, as if the president stopped the bill from becoming a law by keeping it in his or her pocket until Congress stops meeting.

Sometimes it takes years to make a law. Sometimes laws are made in just a few days.

Among the most important laws that Congress makes are laws about money. The government spends a lot of money to perform its many jobs. Congress decides how much money the government may spend each year and in what ways to spend it. This is called the *budget*. Think of the budget as a big pie. Different slices of the budget pie pay for the government's many different jobs.

## THE BUDGET PIE

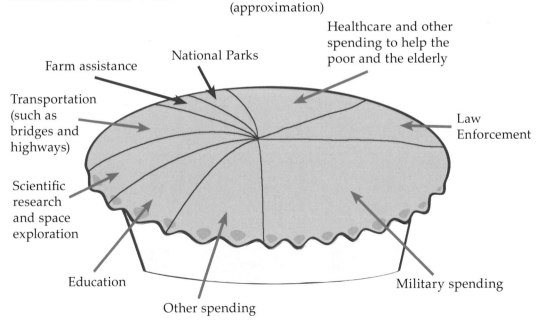

(approximation)

National Parks

Healthcare and other spending to help the poor and the elderly

Farm assistance

Transportation (such as bridges and highways)

Law Enforcement

Scientific research and space exploration

Education

Other spending

Military spending

Congress also makes laws about how the government can raise money. The main way for the government to raise money is from *taxes*, which are payments that citizens, businesses, and other people who live in the U.S. make to the government. Congress decides how much money people and businesses must pay in taxes and when those taxes must be paid.

For example, some taxes are collected from the money that people make when they work. Other taxes are paid when people buy certain products, like gasoline. Usually, the more money someone makes the more money they pay to the government in taxes.

## TAXES PAY FOR THINGS THE GOVERNMENT DOES

The U.S. government uses the money it collects in taxes in many ways. For example, taxes pay for highways, bridges, railroads, and airports. Taxes pay the salaries of people who serve in the military, as well as for their uniforms, ships, airplanes, and other equipment. Doctors and scientists who study ways to prevent and treat diseases are paid with tax money, as are inspectors who test food and drugs to make sure they are safe, and other people who work for the government. The government also uses some tax money to help citizens who do not have enough money for food, medical care, a place to live, or to go to college.

States and local governments, such as cities, counties, and villages, also collect taxes. These taxes pay for schools, libraries, teachers, police officers, and parks, for example.

**D**eciding how much money to put in the budget and how much to collect in taxes may be Congress's most important job. Some citizens want the government to do more even if that means a bigger budget and more taxes. Some citizens want very low taxes and want the government to do less. When citizens decide who they want to elect to Congress and as president, they usually vote for someone who has similar ideas as they do about how much the government should collect in taxes, how much money it should spend, and how it should spend it.

---

**FOR DISCUSSION:** We've described many jobs that the government performs, all of which are paid for by taxes. Some day you will pay taxes. Which of these jobs do you think are most important for the government to spend your tax dollars on? Which ones do you think are least important?

---

**T**he executive branch is responsible for doing most of the jobs that the Constitution gives to the U.S. government. This includes spending the government's money according to the budget that Congress makes, performing the duties that the Constitution and laws give to the executive branch, and making sure that citizens follow the law. The president is in charge of this branch and is sometimes called the *chief executive.*

The executive branch has 15 departments with different responsibilities. The president appoints people to lead each department. A majority of the senators must approve the people that the president selects to lead the departments. Leaders of the executive departments work closely with the president and are called the president's *cabinet.*

Many people work in the executive branch. Some of them *enforce* the laws, which means making sure people obey the laws. For example, the United States has laws about health and safety. To enforce these laws, some workers in the Department of Labor inspect factories to make sure they are safe for the people who work there. Others in the Department of Health and Human Services inspect factories where food is produced to make sure they are clean and the food is safe to eat. Still others in several different departments inspect the water we drink and air we breathe, enforce laws about guns, explosives, and drugs, and make sure people pay taxes. When people do not obey certain laws, called criminal laws, some executive branch workers in the Departments of Justice and other departments are responsible for arresting them, putting them in jail, and bringing them to court.

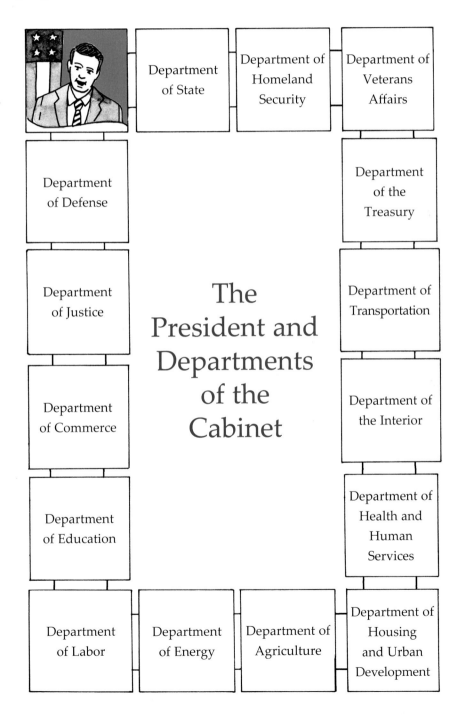

The President and Departments of the Cabinet

- Department of State
- Department of Homeland Security
- Department of Veterans Affairs
- Department of Defense
- Department of the Treasury
- Department of Justice
- Department of Transportation
- Department of Commerce
- Department of the Interior
- Department of Education
- Department of Health and Human Services
- Department of Labor
- Department of Energy
- Department of Agriculture
- Department of Housing and Urban Development

Other people who work in the executive branch provide services and work on projects for the people of the United States. For example, some workers in the Department of Transportation help to build highways and bridges, while some in the Department of Agriculture help farmers learn how to produce more food. Others in the Department of the Interior manage and maintain the national parks and memorials, such as Yellowstone National Park and Mount Rushmore, and help visitors enjoy their visits safely. Doctors and scientists who work in several parts of the government search for ways to cure diseases and work on space exploration. And some of the people who work in the executive branch help people who do not have much money by helping them find jobs, get food, or find a place to live.

**FOR DISCUSSION:** Does a member of your family or someone you know work for the U.S. government or for a state or local government? What do they do? How does the work they do help the citizens of the U.S. or of your state or place you live?

The president has two other important jobs. One is to command all of the men and women in the military. In addition to soldiers, sailors, marines, and pilots, many individuals serve in other positions within the military. Some buy and take care of tanks, airplanes, ships, and other equipment, while others maintain military bases. The military has doctors, teachers, cooks, and truck drivers.

The Constitution gives Congress the power to declare war on another country, but the president can order the military to defend the United States at any time and any place. Everyone who works in the military must be prepared to travel anywhere in the world if they are ordered to go. The Department of Defense manages the military and its offices are in a building called the Pentagon near Washington, D.C.

The president's other important job is to work with leaders of other countries to agree on ways for our country and theirs to work together and get along. Sometimes, the United States helps countries that need military protection from other countries, or provides money, food, or equipment to countries that need help.

The president sometimes meets directly with leaders of other countries. At other times people who work for the president meet with foreign leaders or people who work for them. Some countries want to get along with the United States, some do not. Working with other countries and meeting with their leaders is important for the United States' protection and business interests. Most countries want to work with us. If a country threatens the United

States, however, the president and people who work for the president have to take action to make them stop. The president makes sure the military is always ready to protect us.

The president can also help to make laws. Each year, for example, the president sends Congress a budget plan for how the government should spend its money. The members of Congress examine the president's budget and decide how much of it to make into law and how much of it to change.

The president may also have ideas for new laws, such as tax laws, laws about safety, and other ways the government can help the citizens. The president asks Congress to make these ideas into laws. Sometimes Congress agrees with the president's ideas and sometimes they don't.

Like the members of Congress, the president is elected. Every four years the citizens of the United States have the opportunity

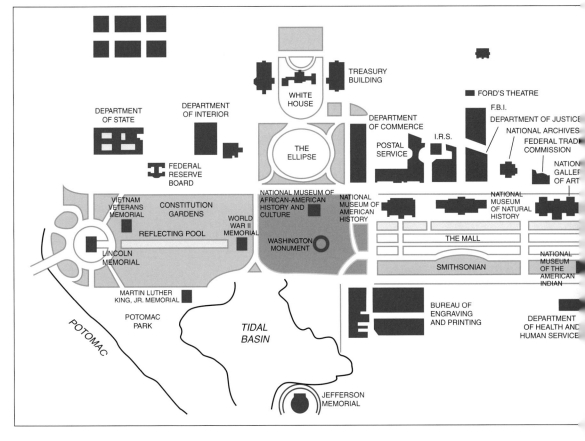

Places to Visit in Washington, D.C.

to choose who they want to be president. Citizens must be 18 or older to vote. The first President of the United States was George Washington. Do you know who the current president is?

# THE CAPITOL AND THE CAPITAL

The president lives in Washington, D.C., in a mansion called the *White House*. The White House is not too far from the U.S. Capitol, where Congress works. Many of the people who work for the U.S. government work in buildings in and near Washington, D.C.

Because the leaders of the government and all of the cabinet departments have their main offices in *Washington, D.C.*, it is called the *capital of the United States*. If you visit Washington, D.C., you will see lots of buildings where people in the U.S. government work.

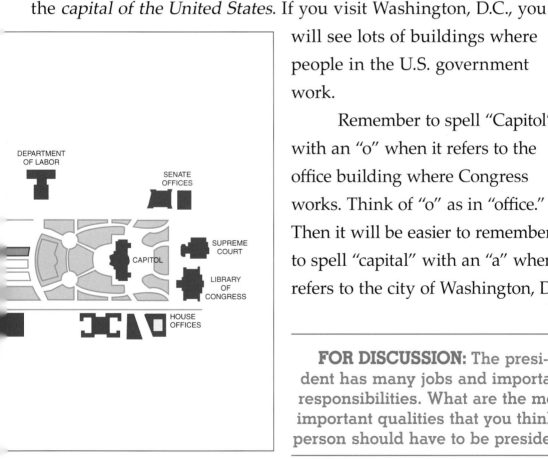

Remember to spell "Capitol" with an "o" when it refers to the office building where Congress works. Think of "o" as in "office." Then it will be easier to remember to spell "capital" with an "a" when it refers to the city of Washington, D.C.

**FOR DISCUSSION:** The president has many jobs and important responsibilities. What are the most important qualities that you think a person should have to be president?

# ★ THE COURTS ★

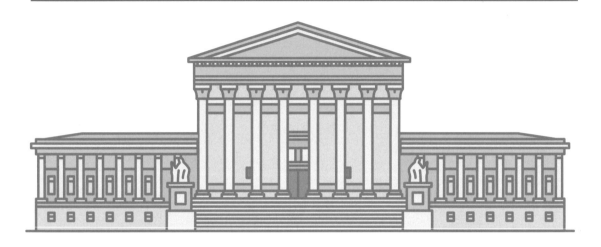

The United States courts do the work of the judicial branch, which is the third branch of the U.S. government. State and local governments also have courts.

Courts are where people go when they have disagreements that involve legal matters. For example, sometimes people disagree with the government about what a law means or about whether the Constitution allows the government to take a particular action. The people and the government go to court, and the court decides how to interpret the law.

Sometimes a person injures another person, damages someone's property, or breaks an agreement. The people go to court, and the court decides who is right and who is wrong and whether someone has to pay for the injury or damage.

Sometimes the government believes that a person has not obeyed a law. The government brings the person to court so the court can decide whether or not that person is guilty of breaking the law. If the court finds that the person is guilty, it also decides on the punishment.

# ★ JUDGES ★

The people in charge of the courts are called *judges*. Judges decide some court cases by themselves. In others, a group of citizens called a jury makes the decision.

Judges of the U.S. courts are not elected, although judges of many state courts are. The president selects men and women to serve as judges of the U.S. courts. Usually, the people who the president picks to become judges have spent many years studying and working with the law. Many U.S. judges used to be judges of state courts. Before a person can become a U.S. judge, the Senate must approve him or her.

The U.S. courts have three levels. The first court that decides a case is called a *U.S. district court*. This is where trials are held. If the loser of a case does not like the decision made by the judge in the district court, he or she can go to another court called a *U.S. court of appeals*, which decides whether the district judge made the correct decision. In some cases, people can go to a third level of court, called the *Supreme Court of the United States*, which has the final say. The Supreme Court building is in Washington, D.C., right across the street from the U.S. Capitol, where Congress works.

---

**FOR DISCUSSION:** Sometimes Congress passes and the president signs a law that many people think is not allowed by the Constitution. When that happens, courts are often asked to decide whether or not the Constitution allows the law. Why is that an important job of the government?

---

# Supreme Court

↑

# U.S. Courts of Appeals

↑

# U.S. District Courts

**Y**ou have learned a lot about how the U.S. government works. You have learned that the U.S. Constitution establishes the U.S. government and provides the rules for what it must do. The Constitution creates three branches of government, which are:

**1** The legislative branch, called the Congress, which makes the laws.

**2** The executive branch, led by the president, which carries out the laws and makes sure the government and the people follow the laws. The president commands the military and works with other countries to protect our country and its citizens.

**3** The judicial branch, consisting of the courts, which resolves disagreements, including disagreements about specific laws. In some cases, courts decide whether or not people have obeyed the law and how to punish them if they have not.

You have learned that citizens elect the members of Congress and the president by voting. The president chooses the judges of the U.S. courts. One of the houses of Congress, called the Senate, must approve the judges that the president selects.

You have learned that people pay taxes so the government has money to do its many jobs. You have also learned that many people work for the government, and many of them do their work in Washington, D.C., which is the capital of the United States.

The people of the United States created the U.S. government and gave it its authority. But the government cannot do its job alone. It depends upon citizens for support in many ways, including:

- Voting to elect the president and members of the House and Senate.
- Paying taxes to pay for the government's work.
- Serving in the military to help protect the country.
- Serving on juries to decide many court cases.

People can also help the government by telling their members of Congress and the president what kind of laws they want and what the government can do to help the people. They can write letters, go to meetings, and gather together in large groups to let the government's leaders know what they want. If citizens don't like what the government is doing, they can vote to elect new people to lead the government and represent them in Congress. If they do like what the government is doing, they can vote to keep them in office. The people give the government its power and the people decide who they want to exercise that power.

## And That's How the U.S. Government Works.

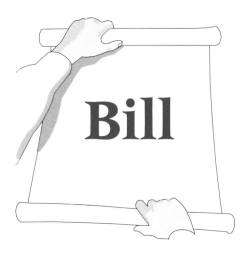

## Bills

Bills are ideas for new laws and suggestions to improve old laws. When a majority of the senators and a majority of the representatives vote to approve a bill, they send the bill to the president. If the president agrees on the terms laid out in the bill, the bill becomes a law. A bill can sometimes become a law even if the president does not agree.

## Branches

Branches are the different parts of the government. The U.S. government has three branches: legislative, executive, and judicial.

## Budget

The budget is the amount of money that Congress allows the government to spend each year. The president gives an annual budget plan to Congress. Congress examines the president's budget and decides which parts to make into law and which parts to change.

## Cabinet

The cabinet consists of the leaders of the fifteen departments in the executive branch who work closely with and advise the president. The president selects the members of the cabinet, but the Senate must approve them.

## Capital of the United States

Washington, D.C., is called the capital of the United States because Congress, the president, and the Supreme Court are all located there, and many other people who work for the U.S. government work in or near Washington, D.C.

## Chief Executive
Chief Executive is another name for the President of the United States, who is the leader of the executive branch of government.

## Citizens
Citizens are people who were born or live in a country or state and have certain rights and duties. For example, a citizen of the United States has the right to vote in an election and the duty to pay taxes.

## Congress of the United States
Congress makes the laws of the United States and does the work of the legislative branch of government. It consists of two groups: The House of Representatives and the Senate. Citizens elect the members of Congress.

## Constitution of the United States
The Constitution contains the rules that created the U.S. government, tells the government what it is supposed to do, and protects the rights of the people.

## Courts
Courts do the work of the judicial branch of government. Courts decide how to resolve disagreements that people cannot settle by themselves, determine whether someone has broken a law and how to punish the person if he or she did, and decide questions about the law and the Constitution.

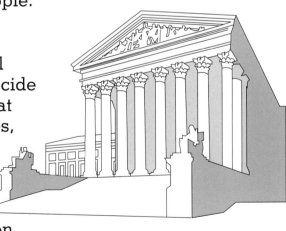

## Democracy
A democracy is a system of government in which people make important decisions by voting, such as electing people to lead the government.

### Election
An election is how the people of a democracy make important decisions. In the United States, for example, citizens who are 18 or older vote to elect members of Congress and the president.

### Executive Branch
The executive branch of government is responsible for enforcing and carrying out the laws that Congress makes. People who work for the executive branch perform jobs such as serving in the military, building roads and bridges, and making sure the air we breathe, water we drink, and food we eat are safe. The President of the United States is the leader of this branch.

### Government
A government performs important jobs for the citizens of a country or state, such as making laws, providing military defense, performing services, and settling disagreements. The U.S. government divides these jobs among three branches: legislative branch, executive branch, and judicial branch.

### Judges
Judges are the people in charge of the courts. Judges of the U.S. courts are not elected, although judges of many state courts are. The president selects men and women to become judges of the U.S. courts, but the Senate must approve them.

JUDGE

## Judicial Branch

The judicial branch of government consists of the courts, which decide how to resolve disagreements that people cannot settle by themselves, determine whether people have broken the law and how to punish them if they did, and decide questions about the law and the Constitution.

## Laws

Laws are rules that the U.S. Congress makes and the president agrees to. Sometimes Congress can make laws even if the president does not agree with the terms of the law. Laws tell the government and the people what they can and cannot do.

## Legislative Branch

The legislative branch of government makes the laws. Congress performs the work of the legislative branch of the U.S. government.

## Military

The U.S. Army, Navy, Air Force, Marine Corps, and Coast Guard are together known as the military. The Department of Defense is in charge of the military, and its offices are in a building called the Pentagon near Washington, D.C.

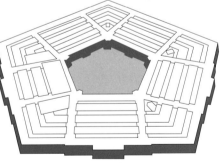

*The Pentagon*

## National Government

A national government performs the work of government for an organized group of states. The U.S. government is the government for the United States of America and makes laws and provides defense and other services for all of the states.

## President of the United States

The president is the leader of the executive branch of government and makes sure the people who work in that branch perform their jobs. The president is the commander of the military and also works and meets with leaders of other countries.

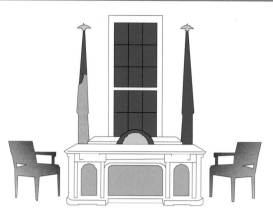

## Representatives

Representatives are people who are chosen to work for the people who elect them. Citizens of the United States elect representatives to work for them in Congress.

## Republic

A type of government that gets its power from the citizens and is led by people whom the citizens elect to represent them.

## Supermajority

A majority that is greater than one-half, such as the two-thirds majority that is required for Congress to pass a bill that the president has vetoed.

## Supreme Court of the United States

The Supreme Court can decide, in some cases, whether other courts made the right decision. It is the highest court in the United States and is located in Washington, D.C.

## Taxes

Taxes are the money that people pay to the government so it can perform the many jobs and responsibilities that the Constitution and the laws give to it.

## U.S. Capitol

The building in Washington, D.C., where Congress meets and does most of its work. The Capitol is an office building, so remember to spell it with an "o" as in "office."

## U.S. Courts of Appeals

The U.S. courts of appeals are the second level of the court system in the United States. When people do not like the decision of a judge in the district court, they can ask a court of appeals to review the decision and decide if it is correct.

## U.S. District Courts

The U.S. district courts are the first level of courts in the U.S. court system and are where trials are held. People who are not satisfied with the decision of a district court can ask a U.S. court of appeals to review the decision and decide if it is correct.

## U.S. House of Representatives

The U.S. House of Representatives is one of the two houses that make up Congress. Members of the House are elected to do their jobs for two years.

## U.S. Senate

The U.S. Senate is one of the two houses that make up Congress. Senators are elected to do their jobs for six years.

## Veto

A veto is when the president does not agree with a bill that Congress has approved and sends it back to Congress. Congress can still make a bill into a law over the president's veto if each house passes the bill again with a two-thirds majority, which is called a supermajority.

41

## Washington, D.C.

Washington, D.C. is the capital of the United States. Congress, the president, and the Supreme Court are all located there, and many other people who work for the U.S. government work in or near Washington, D.C.

## White House

The White House is a mansion in Washington, D.C. and is the home of the president and the president's family. It also has offices for the president and for many of the people who work for the president.

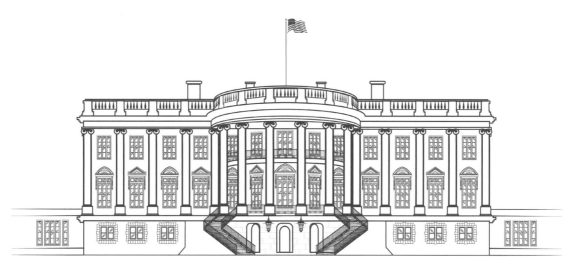

# ★ RESOURCE GUIDE ★

## Books

Many fine children's books are available about the U.S. government. Here are some of them.

Buchanan, Shelly, *Our Government: The Three Branches* (Teacher Created Materials, Huntington Beach, CA, 2014).

Burgan, Michael, *The Branches of the U.S. Government* (Children's Press, Danbury, CT, 2011).

Giesecke, Ernestine, *National Government* (Heinemann, Portsmouth, NH, 2016).

Prior, Jennifer Overend, *You and the U.S. Government* (Teacher Created Materials, Huntington Beach, CA, 2014).

Ragone, Nick, *The Everything American Government Book: From the Constitution to Present-Day Elections, All You Need to Understand Our Democratic System* (Adams Media, Avon, MA, 2004).

Reis, Ronald A., *The U.S. Congress for Kids: Over 200 Years of Lawmaking, Deal-Breaking, and Compromising* (Chicago Review Press, Inc., Chicago, IL, 2014).

## Websites

Here are the addresses of some informative webpages for children about the U.S. government.

Ben's Guide to U.S. Government for Kids (Government Printing Office) *http://bensguide.gpo.gov*

iCivics
*https://www.icivics.org*

Social Studies for Kids
*http://www.socialstudiesforkids.com/subjects/government.htm*

What Is Government? An Intro for Kids from Sanger Academy
*https://www.youtube.com/watch?v=JY7umgfV8gg*

# ★ INDEX ★

## E

## F

## G